Games
for
Wedding
Shower
Fun

by Sharon Dlugosch
and
Florence Nelson

Illustrations by Sandra Knuth

Copyright © 1985 by Sharon E. Dlugosch

Brighton Publications, Inc.
P.O. Box 120706
St. Paul, MN 55112-0706
1-800-536-BOOK (2665)

FIRST EDITION: 1985

PRINTED IN THE UNITED STATES OF AMERICA
LIBRARY OF CONGRESS
CATALOG CARD NUMBER: 83-073600
ISBN: 0-918420-12-1

Contents

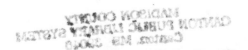

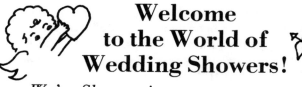

Welcome to the World of Wedding Showers!

We're Showerwise

We know you'd like to create wonderful *memories* for your favorite happy couple . . . the intended bride and groom and we're here to help. Since we co-authored WEDDING SHOWER FUN with Dlugosch and Nelson, they asked us to stick around for an encore. And here it is . . . GAMES FOR WEDDING SHOWER FUN!

We want you to know that this book brings you the very best ideas and games from The-Great-Wedding-Shower-Galaxy, beyond the Milky Way. They're all new and are guaranteed to work for gatherings of singles or couples. We think you'll find them a delightful change of pace and, of course . . . FUN!

There are four new, ready-to-use *WEDDING SHOWER GAMES*, with individual sheets for as many as twelve guests. Just hand them out and start the memories rolling.

You'll also find a sprinkling of games that just require a short explanation from us. Look over our *GAME SPRINKLES* for ideas you can carry out on your own.

And because we just couldn't stop, we've added a few tender touches. Our *MEMORY-MAKERS* will mark YOUR shower as truly special.

So, come on along. Let the games . . . and the fun, begin!

Door Prize Fun

The big news is door prizes! These are surprise presents your guests can win just for attending your shower and helping to make the happy memories. You can use as many of these ideas as you wish. In fact, you may use them all, each at a different moment in the shower. Because they'll add sparkle and variety, you'll want to do it with flair. A drum roll, piano chord or bell will alert your guests to the coming excitement.

First you'll need the name tags we've provided, following the game sheet section. When you use one door prize idea, pre-NUMBER the tags. If you use two ideas, add a LETTER (or two letters if your guests number more than twenty-six). For all three ideas, add a SYMBOL to the number and letter (triangle, bird, hammer, etc.). Simply have guests write their names on the tags and pin or tape them on.

Now you're ready for the prize drawings!

BALLOON BALLYHOO—Use balloons in your decorations, but separate a "balloon bouquet" from the rest. Write numbers (corresponding to those on the name tags) on small pieces of paper. Then fold and insert one into each selected balloon before inflating. At door prize time, ask the bride or groom to choose a balloon from the bouquet, sit on it, and attempt to burst it . . . no hands allowed! It can be done, and usually is to the cheers and ballyhoo of all. The guest with the number found in the balloon wins! Just "pop" again for each door prize, til your bouquet is no more.

SURPRISE WRAP-UP—Write a different letter of the alphabet (corresponding to the name tags) on as many small pieces of paper as you have door prizes. Insert each into a small box and gaily gift wrap. After all shower gifts have been opened, the bride and groom also "give" presents. Ask them to open each box and announce one winner at a time. It's a surprise touch that makes the "gift-ees" givers, too.

CUPCAKE CAPER—Make shower cupcakes. Draw symbols (corresponding to the name tags) on as many small pieces of paper as you have door prizes, and then fold. Before you pop the cupcakes into the oven, tuck a paper in a selected few. Bake and decorate. During refreshments, those who "chew paper" are rewarded with a door prize. You'll be known as the most original baker in town!

NOTE: Prize ideas can be found in the book, WEDDING SHOWER FUN by Sharon E. Dlugosch and Florence E. Nelson, available at gift shops and book stores. Or order this book direct by sending a self-addressed, stamped #10 envelope to Brighton Publications, Inc., to request a booklist and price information.

Game Sprinkles

Skillful Eyeful

Tell your guests they're about to be tested on their powers of observation. Also say that in a few minutes, you're going to ask the bride and groom to leave the room. In the meantime, distribute a sheet of paper and a pencil to each one. Ask them to draw a line down the center of the paper, making two columns, headed "bride" and "groom." After everyone has taken a good look, usher the duo into another room. As an "after-thought" ask the mother or mothers of the couple to keep them company. When the four have left, tell guests to write down as many things as they can remember about each MOTHER (color of dress, shoes, hair, wearing glasses?, etc.). If they let you escape alive, give a prize for the most accurate list.

A Rose . . . Is a Rose . . . Is a Rose

Pass a fresh rose around the room so that each guest has a few seconds to look at it and enjoy its fragrance, while remembering as much as they can about it. When the rose comes back to you, ask your guests to write down the NUMBER OF PETALS in the flower (or keep a tally of who guesses what if you'd rather not pass out pencils and paper). Then request that the bride and groom carefully pluck off each petal, counting as they go, and place them in a small square of netting. When the counting is done, the guest who comes closest to the correct number, wins a prize. For a grand finale, gather the ends of the netting, tie them with a colorful ribbon and present the mini sac to the bride . . . as a rose-petal remembrance sachet.

The Good Ole Days

Before the day of your shower, think back to the year in which the bride and/or groom were born. Develop questions around the newsworthy events of that time. What were the popular songs, radio or TV programs? What movie won the Academy Award? What was the price of hamburgers, cars, coffee? What political events or medical breakthroughs were there? What was invented or discovered? (Your librarian can help you.) At your shower, you can read off one question at a time, after you've distributed paper and pencil, and ask guests to write down their answers on the spot. Or you can type up your questions, make copies, and distribute these. In either case, the guest with the most correct answers wins a prize. Then give your copy (with answers) to the couple as a momento. We bet it'll be "news" to them!

Paper Designer's Surprise

Pass out pencils and sealed envelopes containing one sheet of paper in each. Tell your guests that this is a race. When you give the signal, they're to open their envelope and tear the sheet into the form of a wedding cake. Ask them to sign their paper cake and return it to its envelope. Collect all envelopes and present them to the guests of honor. They get to judge who the winner is on the basis of neatness, trim and tidy appearance, and careful way . . . the ENVELOPE was opened! Have your bags packed so you can leave town if the crowd gets ugly.

Sherlock Holmes Strikes Again

Make up mystery phrases that could describe the well-known stores and restaurants in your area. Pick fifteen or twenty of your favorite local shops and eateries. Then create a riddle-clue for each, as we've done in the following examples:

Lots of cents . . . . _____ (Penny's)
To singe . . . . _____ (Sears)
Had a farm . . . . _____ (McDonald's)

Type or print these as above (without the answers, of course). Make as many copies as needed. Distribute them at game time and ask guests to solve each mystery by filling in the blanks. The best "detective" in the crowd wins a prize.

Memory-Makers

If you have our book, WEDDING SHOWER FUN, you already know we're hopeless, but practical, romantics at heart. So how can we leave you now without something special?

Our MEMORY-MAKERS are the little touches that make your shower just a bit different from any other. Their happy function is to stir up the old emotions . . . the kind that sometimes unite generations, sometimes recall the past, sometimes start a new tradition . . . and every time . . . create deep-down, lasting memories.

Photo Fantasy

Use a corner of your gift or refreshment table to set out wedding photographs of parents, grandparents, aunts, uncles, brothers and sisters of the couple. This visual display serves to link the generations (maybe fill the gap?) and bring family ties into view. The difference in wedding fashions is a good conversation starter, too.

Fashion Display

Ask the mothers of the couple, or preferably the grandmothers, if you might show their bridal dresses and other wedding memorabilia (fans, hair combs, shoes, etc.) at your shower. The gowns should be hung on sewing forms if at all possible and shown in all their glory.

Raise Your Glass

What's a celebration without a toast? Make yours special by composing your very own. A sincere poem, spoken by a close friend or family member can create a mighty warm feeling among all celebrants. Ask a caligrapher to record the toast on fine parchment paper. Mount it in an elegant frame and your words will continue "toasting" the couple for years to come.

Signed Survival Kit

Ask each guest to bring a small essential item, in addition to their shower gift . . . for the couple's "Handy-Box." Tape, string, scissors, flashlight, nails and hammer are a few things that will see them through a good many emergencies. Have guests sign the items with permanent marker . . . a happy reminder, sometime in the future, of family and friends who tried to ease the couple's way.

Your Autograph, Please

Purchase a large dish towel, an embroidery hoop and some colorful textile pens (or thin-lined permanent markers). Move the hoop as needed to provide a firm writing surface. Print the couple's names and the date of your shower in three lines at the top (i.e., Mary and Bob's/Wedding Shower/and the date). Decorate the border with drawn-on flowers, ribbons, wedding shower umbrellas, etc. During your shower, ask each guest to "hoop up" and autograph the towel. How's that for a personalized treasure for the couple's kitchen?

Sachet Bounty

If fresh flowers are a part of your shower decor, a good wind-down activity when your shower's about over is to hold a "petal pluckin' bee" for guests who'd like to linger. Carefully remove all petals from the flowers and place about a handful each in squares of netting. Draw up the sides and tie them with thin satin cording, allowing enough extra cording to be tied later around a closet rod. Attach all sachets, temporarily, to a hanger and present it to the couple. When the petals dry, the sachets can be individually transferred to more permanent homes in the couples closets. And that's what memories are made of!

Ready-To-Use Games

Now as we promised, you'll find four new hassle-free games on the following pages, with game sheets for twelve guests each. Simply tear along the perforations and pass them out. Set your own time limit on the games that require one. Answers can be found on page 111.

Starting Life Together

Unscramble these important wedding words that help make happier marriages. They're all things that money can't buy. The player with the most correct answers in the allotted time is the winner!

You'll find a hint to the meaning of the scrambled word in parenthesis.

1. OVEL (Amour) _____

2. RASHGIN (Doing Your Part) _____

3. RUMOH (Light Heartedness) _____

4. VIIGGN (Contributing) _____

5. GNIRAC (Concern) _____

6. FIEDNRPHSI (Mutual regard) _____

7. FNU (Gleeful Activity) _____

8. MEGOCNREUNETA (Go For It) _____

9. TIENAPEC (Cheerful Tolerance) _____

10. TNOIFECFA (Tender Passion) _____

11. KLIGNAT (Communicating) _____

12. JUSTDANEMT (Adapting) _____

13. USTTR (Believe) _____

14. SOREENGYIT (Open-handedness) _____

15. MENTFFLLLIU (Growth) _____

16. UQLAETIY (Balance) _____

Starting Life Together

Unscramble these important wedding words that help make happier marriages. They're all things that money can't buy. The player with the most correct answers in the allotted time is the winner!

   You'll find a hint to the meaning of the scrambled word in parenthesis.

1. OVEL (Amour) _____

2. RASHGIN (Doing Your Part) _____

3. RUMOH (Light Heartedness) _____

4. VIIGGN (Contributing) _____

5. GNIRAC (Concern) _____

6. FIEDNRPHSI (Mutual regard) _____

7. FNU (Gleeful Activity) _____

8. MEGOCNREUNETA (Go For It) _____

9. TIENAPEC (Cheerful Tolerance) _____

10. TNOIFECFA (Tender Passion) _____

11. KLIGNAT (Communicating) _____

12. JUSTDANEMT (Adapting) _____

13. USTTR (Believe) _____

14. SOREENGYIT (Open-handedness) _____

15. MENTFFLLLIU (Growth) _____

16. UQLAETIY (Balance) _____

Starting Life Together

Unscramble these important wedding words that help make happier marriages. They're all things that money can't buy. The player with the most correct answers in the allotted time is the winner!

You'll find a hint to the meaning of the scrambled word in parenthesis.

1. OVEL (Amour) _____

2. RASHGIN (Doing Your Part) _____

3. RUMOH (Light Heartedness) _____

4. VIIGGN (Contributing) _____

5. GNIRAC (Concern) _____

6. FIEDNRPHSI (Mutual regard) _____

7. FNU (Gleeful Activity) _____

8. MEGOCNREUNETA (Go For It) _____

9. TIENAPEC (Cheerful Tolerance) _____

10. TNOIFECFA (Tender Passion) _____

11. KLIGNAT (Communicating) _____

12. JUSTDANEMT (Adapting) _____

13. USTTR (Believe) _____

14. SOREENGYIT (Open-handedness) _____

15. MENTFFLLLIU (Growth) _____

16. UQLAETIY (Balance) _____

Starting Life Together

Unscramble these important wedding words that help make happier marriages. They're all things that money can't buy. The player with the most correct answers in the allotted time is the winner!

You'll find a hint to the meaning of the scrambled word in parenthesis.

1. OVEL (Amour) _____

2. RASHGIN (Doing Your Part) _____

3. RUMOH (Light Heartedness) _____

4. VIIGGN (Contributing) _____

5. GNIRAC (Concern) _____

6. FIEDNRPHSI (Mutual regard) _____

7. FNU (Gleeful Activity) _____

8. MEGOCNREUNETA (Go For It) _____

9. TIENAPEC (Cheerful Tolerance) _____

10. TNOIFECFA (Tender Passion) _____

11. KLIGNAT (Communicating) _____

12. JUSTDANEMT (Adapting) _____

13. USTTR (Believe) _____

14. SOREENGYIT (Open-handedness) _____

15. MENTFFLLLIU (Growth) _____

16. UQLAETIY (Balance) _____

Starting Life Together

Unscramble these important wedding words that help make happier marriages. They're all things that money can't buy. The player with the most correct answers in the allotted time is the winner!

You'll find a hint to the meaning of the scrambled word in parenthesis.

1. OVEL (Amour) _____

2. RASHGIN (Doing Your Part) _____

3. RUMOH (Light Heartedness) _____

4. VIIGGN (Contributing) _____

5. GNIRAC (Concern) _____

6. FIEDNRPHSI (Mutual regard) _____

7. FNU (Gleeful Activity) _____

8. MEGOCNREUNETA (Go For It) _____

9. TIENAPEC (Cheerful Tolerance) _____

10. TNOIFECFA (Tender Passion) _____

11. KLIGNAT (Communicating) _____

12. JUSTDANEMT (Adapting) _____

13. USTTR (Believe) _____

14. SOREENGYIT (Open-handedness) _____

15. MENTFFLLLIU (Growth) _____

16. UQLAETIY (Balance) _____

Starting Life Together

Unscramble these important wedding words that help make happier marriages. They're all things that money can't buy. The player with the most correct answers in the allotted time is the winner!

You'll find a hint to the meaning of the scrambled word in parenthesis.

1. OVEL (Amour) _____

2. RASHGIN (Doing Your Part) _____

3. RUMOH (Light Heartedness) _____

4. VIIGGN (Contributing) _____

5. GNIRAC (Concern) _____

6. FIEDNRPHSI (Mutual regard) _____

7. FNU (Gleeful Activity) _____

8. MEGOCNREUNETA (Go For It) _____

9. TIENAPEC (Cheerful Tolerance) _____

10. TNOIFECFA (Tender Passion) _____

11. KLIGNAT (Communicating) _____

12. JUSTDANEMT (Adapting) _____

13. USTTR (Believe) _____

14. SOREENGYIT (Open-handedness) _____

15. MENTFFLLLIU (Growth) _____

16. UQLAETIY (Balance) _____

Starting Life Together

Unscramble these important wedding words that help make happier marriages. They're all things that money can't buy. The player with the most correct answers in the allotted time is the winner!

You'll find a hint to the meaning of the scrambled word in parenthesis.

1. OVEL (Amour) _____

2. RASHGIN (Doing Your Part) _____

3. RUMOH (Light Heartedness) _____

4. VIIGGN (Contributing) _____

5. GNIRAC (Concern) _____

6. FIEDNRPHSI (Mutual regard) _____

7. FNU (Gleeful Activity) _____

8. MEGOCNREUNETA (Go For It) _____

9. TIENAPEC (Cheerful Tolerance) _____

10. TNOIFECFA (Tender Passion) _____

11. KLIGNAT (Communicating) _____

12. JUSTDANEMT (Adapting) _____

13. USTTR (Believe) _____

14. SOREENGYIT (Open-handedness) _____

15. MENTFFLLLIU (Growth) _____

16. UQLAETIY (Balance) _____

Starting Life Together

Unscramble these important wedding words that help make happier marriages. They're all things that money can't buy. The player with the most correct answers in the allotted time is the winner!

You'll find a hint to the meaning of the scrambled word in parenthesis.

1. OVEL (Amour) _____

2. RASHGIN (Doing Your Part) _____

3. RUMOH (Light Heartedness) _____

4. VIIGGN (Contributing) _____

5. GNIRAC (Concern) _____

6. FIEDNRPHSI (Mutual regard) _____

7. FNU (Gleeful Activity) _____

8. MEGOCNREUNETA (Go For It) _____

9. TIENAPEC (Cheerful Tolerance) _____

10. TNOIFECFA (Tender Passion) _____

11. KLIGNAT (Communicating) _____

12. JUSTDANEMT (Adapting) _____

13. USTTR (Believe) _____

14. SOREENGYIT (Open-handedness) _____

15. MENTFFLLLIU (Growth) _____

16. UQLAETIY (Balance) _____

Starting Life Together

Unscramble these important wedding words that help make happier marriages. They're all things that money can't buy. The player with the most correct answers in the allotted time is the winner!

    You'll find a hint to the meaning of the scrambled word in parenthesis.

1. OVEL (Amour) _____

2. RASHGIN (Doing Your Part) _____

3. RUMOH (Light Heartedness) _____

4. VIIGGN (Contributing) _____

5. GNIRAC (Concern) _____

6. FIEDNRPHSI (Mutual regard) _____

7. FNU (Gleeful Activity) _____

8. MEGOCNREUNETA (Go For It) _____

9. TIENAPEC (Cheerful Tolerance) _____

10. TNOIFECFA (Tender Passion) _____

11. KLIGNAT (Communicating) _____

12. JUSTDANEMT (Adapting) _____

13. USTTR (Believe) _____

14. SOREENGYIT (Open-handedness) _____

15. MENTFFLLLIU (Growth) _____

16. UQLAETIY (Balance) _____

Starting Life Together

Unscramble these important wedding words that help make happier marriages. They're all things that money can't buy. The player with the most correct answers in the allotted time is the winner!

You'll find a hint to the meaning of the scrambled word in parenthesis.

1. OVEL (Amour) _____

2. RASHGIN (Doing Your Part) _____

3. RUMOH (Light Heartedness) _____

4. VIIGGN (Contributing) _____

5. GNIRAC (Concern) _____

6. FIEDNRPHSI (Mutual regard) _____

7. FNU (Gleeful Activity) _____

8. MEGOCNREUNETA (Go For It) _____

9. TIENAPEC (Cheerful Tolerance) _____

10. TNOIFECFA (Tender Passion) _____

11. KLIGNAT (Communicating) _____

12. JUSTDANEMT (Adapting) _____

13. USTTR (Believe) _____

14. SOREENGYIT (Open-handedness) _____

15. MENTFFLLLIU (Growth) _____

16. UQLAETIY (Balance) _____

Starting Life Together

Unscramble these important wedding words that help make happier marriages. They're all things that money can't buy. The player with the most correct answers in the allotted time is the winner!

You'll find a hint to the meaning of the scrambled word in parenthesis.

1. OVEL (Amour) _____

2. RASHGIN (Doing Your Part) _____

3. RUMOH (Light Heartedness) _____

4. VIIGGN (Contributing) _____

5. GNIRAC (Concern) _____

6. FIEDNRPHSI (Mutual regard) _____

7. FNU (Gleeful Activity) _____

8. MEGOCNREUNETA (Go For It) _____

9. TIENAPEC (Cheerful Tolerance) _____

10. TNOIFECFA (Tender Passion) _____

11. KLIGNAT (Communicating) _____

12. JUSTDANEMT (Adapting) _____

13. USTTR (Believe) _____

14. SOREENGYIT (Open-handedness) _____

15. MENTFFLLLIU (Growth) _____

16. UQLAETIY (Balance) _____

Starting Life Together

Unscramble these important wedding words that help make happier marriages. They're all things that money can't buy. The player with the most correct answers in the allotted time is the winner!

You'll find a hint to the meaning of the scrambled word in parenthesis.

1. OVEL (Amour) _____

2. RASHGIN (Doing Your Part) _____

3. RUMOH (Light Heartedness) _____

4. VIIGGN (Contributing) _____

5. GNIRAC (Concern) _____

6. FIEDNRPHSI (Mutual regard) _____

7. FNU (Gleeful Activity) _____

8. MEGOCNREUNETA (Go For It) _____

9. TIENAPEC (Cheerful Tolerance) _____

10. TNOIFECFA (Tender Passion) _____

11. KLIGNAT (Communicating) _____

12. JUSTDANEMT (Adapting) _____

13. USTTR (Believe) _____

14. SOREENGYIT (Open-handedness) _____

15. MENTFFLLLIU (Growth) _____

16. UQLAETIY (Balance) _____

Symbol Sayings

Write the word for each symbol on the line underneath it.

_____   _____   _____

_____   _____   _____   _____

Then fill in the blanks below with the missing word clues. The first guest to complete the list is the winner. So when you're done, shout it out!

You gotta have _____. Sound as a _____. _____ of gab. _____ up the curtain. _____ and tell. Hearts and _____. You take the _____. _____ing don't last, cookery do. For whom the _____s toll. To wear one's _____ on one's sleeve. _____ling, Barnum & Bailey. A _____ for Adano. It's not the _____, it's the thought. _____ of the field. It's a piece of _____. Absence makes the _____ grow fonder. Good sense is the _____ of heaven. _____ around the collar. _____ walk. Say it with _____. Peg 'O My _____. _____in' cousins. _____e of the ball. Love and _____es. Double _____ ceremony.

Symbol Sayings

Write the word for each symbol on the line underneath it.

_____ _____ _____

_____ _____ _____ _____

Then fill in the blanks below with the missing word clues. The first guest to complete the list is the winner. So when you're done, shout it out!

You gotta have _____. Sound as a _____. _____ of gab. _____ up the curtain. _____ and tell. Hearts and _____. You take the _____. _____ing don't last, cookery do. For whom the _____s toll. To wear one's _____ on one's sleeve. _____ling, Barnum & Bailey. A _____ for Adano. It's not the _____, it's the thought. _____ of the field. It's a piece of _____. Absence makes the _____ grow fonder. Good sense is the _____ of heaven. _____ around the collar. _____ walk. Say it with _____. Peg 'O My _____. _____in' cousins. _____e of the ball. Love and _____es. Double _____ ceremony.

Symbol Sayings

Write the word for each symbol on the line underneath it.

_____   _____   _____

_____   _____   _____   _____

Then fill in the blanks below with the missing word clues. The first guest to complete the list is the winner. So when you're done, shout it out!

You gotta have _____. Sound as a _____. _____ of gab. _____ up the curtain. _____ and tell. Hearts and _____. You take the _____. _____ing don't last, cookery do. For whom the _____s toll. To wear one's _____ on one's sleeve. _____ling, Barnum & Bailey. A _____ for Adano. It's not the _____, it's the thought. _____ of the field. It's a piece of _____. Absence makes the _____ grow fonder. Good sense is the _____ of heaven. _____ around the collar. _____ walk. Say it with _____. Peg 'O My _____. _____in' cousins. _____e of the ball. Love and _____es. Double _____ ceremony.

Symbol Sayings

Write the word for each symbol on the line underneath it.

_____   _____   _____

_____   _____   _____   _____

Then fill in the blanks below with the missing word clues. The first guest to complete the list is the winner. So when you're done, shout it out!

You gotta have _____. Sound as a _____. _____ of gab. _____ up the curtain. _____ and tell. Hearts and _____. You take the _____. _____ing don't last, cookery do. For whom the _____s toll. To wear one's _____ on one's sleeve. _____ling, Barnum & Bailey. A _____ for Adano. It's not the _____, it's the thought. _____ of the field. It's a piece of _____. Absence makes the _____ grow fonder. Good sense is the _____ of heaven. _____ around the collar. _____ walk. Say it with _____. Peg 'O My _____. _____in' cousins. _____e of the ball. Love and _____es. Double _____ ceremony.

Symbol Sayings

Write the word for each symbol on the line underneath it.

_____   _____   _____

_____   _____   _____   _____

Then fill in the blanks below with the missing word clues. The first guest to complete the list is the winner. So when you're done, shout it out!

You gotta have _____. Sound as a _____. _____ of gab. _____ up the curtain. _____ and tell. Hearts and _____. You take the _____. _____ing don't last, cookery do. For whom the _____s toll. To wear one's _____ on one's sleeve. _____ling, Barnum & Bailey. A _____ for Adano. It's not the _____, it's the thought. _____ of the field. It's a piece of _____. Absence makes the _____ grow fonder. Good sense is the _____ of heaven. _____ around the collar. _____ walk. Say it with _____. Peg 'O My _____. _____in' cousins. _____e of the ball. Love and _____es. Double _____ ceremony.

Symbol Sayings

Write the word for each symbol on the line underneath it.

_____   _____   _____

_____   _____   _____   _____

Then fill in the blanks below with the missing word clues. The
first guest to complete the list is the winner. So when you're
done, shout it out!

You gotta have _____. Sound as a _____. _____ of
gab. _____ up the curtain. _____ and tell. Hearts and
_____. You take the _____. _____ing don't last,
cookery do. For whom the _____s toll. To wear one's
_____ on one's sleeve. _____ling, Barnum & Bailey. A
_____ for Adano. It's not the _____, it's the thought.
_____ of the field. It's a piece of _____. Absence makes
the _____ grow fonder. Good sense is the _____ of
heaven. _____ around the collar. _____ walk. Say it with
_____. Peg 'O My _____. _____in' cousins.
_____e of the ball. Love and _____es. Double _____
ceremony.

Symbol Sayings

Write the word for each symbol on the line underneath it.

_____   _____   _____

_____   _____   _____   _____

Then fill in the blanks below with the missing word clues. The first guest to complete the list is the winner. So when you're done, shout it out!

You gotta have _____. Sound as a _____. _____ of gab. _____ up the curtain. _____ and tell. Hearts and _____. You take the _____. _____ing don't last, cookery do. For whom the _____s toll. To wear one's _____ on one's sleeve. _____ling, Barnum & Bailey. A _____ for Adano. It's not the _____, it's the thought. _____ of the field. It's a piece of _____. Absence makes the _____ grow fonder. Good sense is the _____ of heaven. _____ around the collar. _____ walk. Say it with _____. Peg 'O My _____. _____in' cousins. _____e of the ball. Love and _____es. Double _____ ceremony.

Symbol Sayings

Write the word for each symbol on the line underneath it.

———— ———— ————

———— ———— ———— ————

Then fill in the blanks below with the missing word clues. The first guest to complete the list is the winner. So when you're done, shout it out!

You gotta have _____. Sound as a _____. _____ of gab. _____ up the curtain. _____ and tell. Hearts and _____. You take the _____. _____ing don't last, cookery do. For whom the _____s toll. To wear one's _____ on one's sleeve. _____ling, Barnum & Bailey. A _____ for Adano. It's not the _____, it's the thought. _____ of the field. It's a piece of _____. Absence makes the _____ grow fonder. Good sense is the _____ of heaven. _____ around the collar. _____ walk. Say it with _____. Peg 'O My _____. _____in' cousins. _____e of the ball. Love and _____es. Double _____ ceremony.

Symbol Sayings

Write the word for each symbol on the line underneath it.

_____   _____   _____

_____   _____   _____   _____

Then fill in the blanks below with the missing word clues. The first guest to complete the list is the winner. So when you're done, shout it out!

You gotta have _____. Sound as a _____. _____ of gab. _____ up the curtain. _____ and tell. Hearts and _____. You take the _____. _____ing don't last, cookery do. For whom the _____s toll. To wear one's _____ on one's sleeve. _____ling, Barnum & Bailey. A _____ for Adano. It's not the _____, it's the thought. _____ of the field. It's a piece of _____. Absence makes the _____ grow fonder. Good sense is the _____ of heaven. _____ around the collar. _____ walk. Say it with _____. Peg 'O My _____. _____in' cousins. _____e of the ball. Love and _____es. Double _____ ceremony.

Symbol Sayings

Write the word for each symbol on the line underneath it.

_____   _____   _____

_____   _____   _____   _____

Then fill in the blanks below with the missing word clues. The first guest to complete the list is the winner. So when you're done, shout it out!

You gotta have _____. Sound as a _____. _____ of gab. _____ up the curtain. _____ and tell. Hearts and _____. You take the _____. _____ing don't last, cookery do. For whom the _____s toll. To wear one's _____ on one's sleeve. _____ling, Barnum & Bailey. A _____ for Adano. It's not the _____, it's the thought. _____ of the field. It's a piece of _____. Absence makes the _____ grow fonder. Good sense is the _____ of heaven. _____ around the collar. _____ walk. Say it with _____. Peg 'O My _____. _____in' cousins. _____e of the ball. Love and _____es. Double _____ ceremony.

Symbol Sayings

Write the word for each symbol on the line underneath it.

Then fill in the blanks below with the missing word clues. The first guest to complete the list is the winner. So when you're done, shout it out!

You gotta have _____. Sound as a _____. _____ of gab. _____ up the curtain. _____ and tell. Hearts and _____. You take the _____. _____ing don't last, cookery do. For whom the _____s toll. To wear one's _____ on one's sleeve. _____ling, Barnum & Bailey. A _____ for Adano. It's not the _____, it's the thought. _____ of the field. It's a piece of _____. Absence makes the _____ grow fonder. Good sense is the _____ of heaven. _____ around the collar. _____ walk. Say it with _____. Peg 'O My _____. _____in' cousins. _____e of the ball. Love and _____es. Double _____ ceremony.

Symbol Sayings

Write the word for each symbol on the line underneath it.

_____ _____ _____

_____ _____ _____ _____

Then fill in the blanks below with the missing word clues. The first guest to complete the list is the winner. So when you're done, shout it out!

You gotta have _____. Sound as a _____. _____ of gab. _____ up the curtain. _____ and tell. Hearts and _____. You take the _____. _____ing don't last, cookery do. For whom the _____s toll. To wear one's _____ on one's sleeve. _____ling, Barnum & Bailey. A _____ for Adano. It's not the _____, it's the thought. _____ of the field. It's a piece of _____. Absence makes the _____ grow fonder. Good sense is the _____ of heaven. _____ around the collar. _____ walk. Say it with _____. Peg 'O My _____. _____in' cousins. _____e of the ball. Love and _____es. Double _____ ceremony.

Courtship and Wedding Word-Puzzle

All of the words below are hidden in this cryptogram. Words go up, down, forward, backward, and diagonally across. Draw a circle around those you find. Player with the most correct answers in the allotted time wins!

HINT: We'll get you started with a "HUG"

Wedding	Bouquet
Bridegroom	Old
Bride	New
Ring	Horn
Honeymoon	Confetti
Flowers	Bell
Shower	Woo
Vows	Date
Heart	Love
Roses	Kiss
Aisle	Hug
Usher	Glove
Ceremony	Ribbons
Rice	Bow
Garter	Marry
I Do	Toast
Honey	Dear

```
B R I D E Z L S M O N
E R L B K W S N P S O
L Y I O G U H O W A O
L V T D V Z O B E G M
R E T I E E W B N T Y
E C E R C G E I Q O E
T I F E M A R R Y A N
R R N H D F O O J S O
A R O S E S D L O T H
G I C U E A K A U M G
K I S S P R N T M N
X D A L R S A T E E I
Y N O M E R E C U Y D
K I P W W D D A Q E D
N R O H O O T Y U N E
E E V O L G B Z O O W
V O W S F T G A B H P
```

Courtship and Wedding Word-Puzzle

All of the words below are hidden in this cryptogram. Words go up, down, forward, backward, and diagonally across. Draw a circle around those you find. Player with the most correct answers in the allotted time wins!

HINT: We'll get you started with a "HUG"

Wedding	Bouquet
Bridegroom	Old
Bride	New
Ring	Horn
Honeymoon	Confetti
Flowers	Bell
Shower	Woo
Vows	Date
Heart	Love
Roses	Kiss
Aisle	Hug
Usher	Glove
Ceremony	Ribbons
Rice	Bow
Garter	Marry
I Do	Toast
Honey	Dear

```
B R I D E Z L S M O N
E R L B K W S N P S O
L Y I O G U H O W A O
L V T D V Z O B E G M
R E T I E E W B N T Y
E C E R C G E I Q O E
T I F E M A R R Y A N
R R N H D F O O J S O
A R O S E S D L O T H
G I C U E A K A U M G
K I S S S P R N T M N
X D A L R S A T E E I
Y N O M E R E C U Y D
K I P W W D D A Q E D
N R O H O O T Y U N E
E E V O L G B Z O O W
V O W S F T G A B H P
```

Courtship and Wedding Word-Puzzle

All of the words below are hidden in this cryptogram. Words go up, down, forward, backward, and diagonally across. Draw a circle around those you find. Player with the most correct answers in the allotted time wins!

HINT: We'll get you started with a "HUG"

Wedding	Bouquet
Bridegroom	Old
Bride	New
Ring	Horn
Honeymoon	Confetti
Flowers	Bell
Shower	Woo
Vows	Date
Heart	Love
Roses	Kiss
Aisle	Hug
Usher	Glove
Ceremony	Ribbons
Rice	Bow
Garter	Marry
I Do	Toast
Honey	Dear

```
B R I D E Z L S M O N
E R L B K W S N P S O
L Y I O G U H O W A O
L V T D V Z O B E G M
R E T I E E W B N T Y
E C E R C G E I Q O E
T I F E M A R R Y A N
R R N H D F O O J S O
A R O S E S D L O T H
G I C U E A K A U M G
K I S S S P R N T M N
X D A L R S A T E E I
Y N O M E R E C U Y D
K I P W W D D A Q E D
N R O H O O T Y U N E
E E V O L G B Z O O W
V O W S F T G A B H P
```

Courtship and Wedding Word-Puzzle

All of the words below are hidden in this cryptogram. Words go up, down, forward, backward, and diagonally across. Draw a circle around those you find. Player with the most correct answers in the allotted time wins!

HINT: We'll get you started with a "HUG"

Wedding	Bouquet		
Bridegroom	Old		
Bride	New		
Ring	Horn		
Honeymoon	Confetti		
Flowers	Bell		
Shower	Woo		
Vows	Date		
Heart	Love		
Roses	Kiss		
Aisle	Hug		
Usher	Glove		
Ceremony	Ribbons		
Rice	Bow		
Garter	Marry		
I Do	Toast		
Honey	Dear		

```
B R I D E Z L S M O N
E R L B K W S N P S O
L Y I O G U H O W A O
L V T D V Z O B E G M
R E T I E E W B N T Y
E C E R C G E I Q O E
T I F E M A R R Y A N
R R N H D F O O J S O
A R O S E S D L O T H
G I C U E A K A U M G
K I S S S P R N T M N
X D A L R S A T E E I
Y N O M E R E C U Y D
K I P W W D D A Q E D
N R O H O O T Y U N E
E E V O L G B Z O O W
V O W S F T G A B H P
```

Courtship and Wedding Word-Puzzle

All of the words below are hidden in this cryptogram. Words go up, down, forward, backward, and diagonally across. Draw a circle around those you find. Player with the most correct answers in the allotted time wins!

HINT: We'll get you started with a "HUG"

Wedding	Bouquet
Bridegroom	Old
Bride	New
Ring	Horn
Honeymoon	Confetti
Flowers	Bell
Shower	Woo
Vows	Date
Heart	Love
Roses	Kiss
Aisle	Hug
Usher	Glove
Ceremony	Ribbons
Rice	Bow
Garter	Marry
I Do	Toast
Honey	Dear

```
B R I D E Z L S M O N
E R L B K W S N P S O
L Y I O G U H O W A O
L V T D V Z O B E G M
R E T I E E W B N T Y
E C E R C G E I Q O E
T I F E M A R R Y A N
R R N H D F O O J S O
A R O S E S D L O T H
G I C U E A K A U M G
K I S S S P R N T M N
X D A L R S A T E E I
Y N O M E R E C U Y D
K I P W W D D A Q E D
N R O H O O T Y U N E
E E V O L G B Z O O W
V O W S F T G A B H P
```

Courtship and Wedding Word-Puzzle

All of the words below are hidden in this cryptogram. Words go up, down, forward, backward, and diagonally across. Draw a circle around those you find. Player with the most correct answers in the allotted time wins!

HINT: We'll get you started with a "HUG"

Wedding	Bouquet
Bridegroom	Old
Bride	New
Ring	Horn
Honeymoon	Confetti
Flowers	Bell
Shower	Woo
Vows	Date
Heart	Love
Roses	Kiss
Aisle	Hug
Usher	Glove
Ceremony	Ribbons
Rice	Bow
Garter	Marry
I Do	Toast
Honey	Dear

```
B R I D E Z L S M O N
E R L B K W S N P S O
L Y I O G U H O W A O
L V T D V Z O B E G M
R E T I E E W B N T Y
E C E R C G E I Q O E
T I F E M A R R Y A N
R R N H D F O O J S O
A R O S E S D L O T H
G I C U E A K A U M G
K I S S S P R N T M N
X D A L R S A T E E I
Y N O M E R E C U Y D
K I P W W D D A Q E D
N R O H O O T Y U N E
E E V O L G B Z O O W
V O W S F T G A B H P
```

Courtship and Wedding Word-Puzzle

All of the words below are hidden in this cryptogram. Words go up, down, forward, backward, and diagonally across. Draw a circle around those you find. Player with the most correct answers in the allotted time wins!

HINT: We'll get you started with a "HUG"

Wedding	Bouquet	B R I D E Z L S M O N
Bridegroom	Old	E R L B K W S N P S O
Bride	New	L Y I O G U H O W A O
Ring	Horn	L V T D V Z O B E G M
Honeymoon	Confetti	R E T I E E W B N T Y
Flowers	Bell	E C E R C G E I Q O E
Shower	Woo	T I F E M A R R Y A N
Vows	Date	R R N H D F O O J S O
Heart	Love	A R O S E S D L O T H
Roses	Kiss	G I C U E A K A U M G
Aisle	Hug	K I S S P R N T M N
Usher	Glove	X D A L R S A T E E I
Ceremony	Ribbons	Y N O M E R E C U Y D
Rice	Bow	K I P W W D D A Q E D
Garter	Marry	N R O H O O T Y U N E
I Do	Toast	E E V O L G B Z O O W
Honey	Dear	V O W S F T G A B H P

Courtship and Wedding Word-Puzzle

All of the words below are hidden in this cryptogram. Words go up, down, forward, backward, and diagonally across. Draw a circle around those you find. Player with the most correct answers in the allotted time wins!

HINT: We'll get you started with a "HUG"

Wedding	Bouquet	B	R	I	D	E	Z	L	S	M	O	N
Bridegroom	Old	E	R	L	B	K	W	S	N	P	S	O
Bride	New	L	Y	I	O	G	U	H	O	W	A	O
Ring	Horn	L	V	T	D	V	Z	O	B	E	G	M
Honeymoon	Confetti	R	E	T	I	E	E	W	B	N	T	Y
Flowers	Bell	E	C	E	R	C	G	E	I	Q	O	E
Shower	Woo	T	I	F	E	M	A	R	R	Y	A	N
Vows	Date	R	R	N	H	D	F	O	O	J	S	O
Heart	Love	A	R	O	S	E	S	D	L	O	T	H
Roses	Kiss	G	I	C	U	E	A	K	A	U	M	G
Aisle	Hug	K	I	S	S	S	P	R	N	T	M	N
Usher	Glove	X	D	A	L	R	S	A	T	E	E	I
Ceremony	Ribbons	Y	N	O	M	E	R	E	C	U	Y	D
Rice	Bow	K	I	P	W	W	D	D	A	Q	E	D
Garter	Marry	N	R	O	H	O	O	T	Y	U	N	E
I Do	Toast	E	E	V	O	L	G	B	Z	O	O	W
Honey	Dear	V	O	W	S	F	T	G	A	B	H	P

Courtship and Wedding Word-Puzzle

All of the words below are hidden in this cryptogram. Words go up, down, forward, backward, and diagonally across. Draw a circle around those you find. Player with the most correct answers in the allotted time wins!

HINT: We'll get you started with a "HUG"

Wedding	Bouquet
Bridegroom	Old
Bride	New
Ring	Horn
Honeymoon	Confetti
Flowers	Bell
Shower	Woo
Vows	Date
Heart	Love
Roses	Kiss
Aisle	Hug
Usher	Glove
Ceremony	Ribbons
Rice	Bow
Garter	Marry
I Do	Toast
Honey	Dear

```
B R I D E Z L S M O N
E R L B K W S N P S O
L Y I O G U H O W A O
L V T D V Z O B E G M
R E T I E E W B N T Y
E C E R C G E I Q O E
T I F E M A R R Y A N
R R N H D F O O J S O
A R O S E S D L O T H
G I C U E A K A U M G
K I S S S P R N T M N
X D A L R S A T E E I
Y N O M E R E C U Y D
K I P W W D D A Q E D
N R O H O O T Y U N E
E E V O L G B Z O O W
V O W S F T G A B H P
```

Courtship and Wedding Word-Puzzle

All of the words below are hidden in this cryptogram. Words go up, down, forward, backward, and diagonally across. Draw a circle around those you find. Player with the most correct answers in the allotted time wins!

HINT: We'll get you started with a "HUG"

Wedding	Bouquet	
Bridegroom	Old	
Bride	New	
Ring	Horn	
Honeymoon	Confetti	
Flowers	Bell	
Shower	Woo	
Vows	Date	
Heart	Love	
Roses	Kiss	
Aisle	Hug	
Usher	Glove	
Ceremony	Ribbons	
Rice	Bow	
Garter	Marry	
I Do	Toast	
Honey	Dear	

```
B R I D E Z L S M O N
E R L B K W S N P S O
L Y I O G U H O W A O
L V T D V Z O B E G M
R E T I E E W B N T Y
E C E R C G E I Q O E
T I F E M A R R Y A N
R R N H D F O O J S O
A R O S E S D L O T H
G I C U E A K A U M G
K I S S S P R N T M N
X D A L R S A T E E I
Y N O M E R E C U Y D
K I P W W D D A Q E D
N R O H O O T Y U N E
E E V O L G B Z O O W
V O W S F T G A B H P
```

Courtship and Wedding Word-Puzzle

All of the words below are hidden in this cryptogram. Words go up, down, forward, backward, and diagonally across. Draw a circle around those you find. Player with the most correct answers in the allotted time wins!

HINT: We'll get you started with a "HUG"

Wedding	Bouquet	
Bridegroom	Old	
Bride	New	
Ring	Horn	
Honeymoon	Confetti	
Flowers	Bell	
Shower	Woo	
Vows	Date	
Heart	Love	
Roses	Kiss	
Aisle	Hug	
Usher	Glove	
Ceremony	Ribbons	
Rice	Bow	
Garter	Marry	
I Do	Toast	
Honey	Dear	

```
B R I D E Z L S M O N
E R L B K W S N P S O
L Y I O G U H O W A O
L V T D V Z O B E G M
R E T I E E W B N T Y
E C E R C G E I Q O E
T I F E M A R R Y A N
R R N H D F O O J S O
A R O S E S D L O T H
G I C U E A K A U M G
K I S S S P R N T M N
X D A L R S A T E E I
Y N O M E R E C U Y D
K I P W W D D A Q E D
N R O H O O T Y U N E
E E V O L G B Z O O W
V O W S F T G A B H P
```

Courtship and Wedding Word-Puzzle

All of the words below are hidden in this cryptogram. Words go up, down, forward, backward, and diagonally across. Draw a circle around those you find. Player with the most correct answers in the allotted time wins!

HINT: We'll get you started with a "HUG"

Wedding	Bouquet	B	R	I	D	E	Z	L	S	M	O	N
Bridegroom	Old	E	R	L	B	K	W	S	N	P	S	O
Bride	New	L	Y	I	O	G	U	H	O	W	A	O
Ring	Horn	L	V	T	D	V	Z	O	B	E	G	M
Honeymoon	Confetti	R	E	T	I	E	E	W	B	N	T	Y
Flowers	Bell	E	C	E	R	C	G	E	I	Q	O	E
Shower	Woo	T	I	F	E	M	A	R	R	Y	A	N
Vows	Date	R	R	N	H	D	F	O	O	J	S	O
Heart	Love	A	R	O	S	E	S	D	L	O	T	H
Roses	Kiss	G	I	C	U	E	A	K	A	U	M	G
Aisle	Hug	K	I	S	S	S	P	R	N	T	M	N
Usher	Glove	X	D	A	L	R	S	A	T	E	E	I
Ceremony	Ribbons	Y	N	O	M	E	R	E	C	U	Y	D
Rice	Bow	K	I	P	W	W	D	D	A	Q	E	D
Garter	Marry	N	R	O	H	O	O	T	Y	U	N	E
I Do	Toast	E	E	V	O	L	G	B	Z	O	O	W
Honey	Dear	V	O	W	S	F	T	G	A	B	H	P

Let's Get the Couple Started!

Write down items, under each of the following headings, that the new bride and groom will need to get their lives going (no duplicates). The player with the most complete list is the winner. Now really concentrate because all game sheets will be given to the couple as a "guide" . . . to get them started!
You'll find a hint under each heading.

KITCHEN	**LIVING ROOM**
Can Opener	*Picture Hangers*

BEDROOM/BATH	**TOOLS/HANDY ITEMS**
Facial Tissue	*Masking Tape*

Let's Get the Couple Started!

Write down items, under each of the following headings, that the new bride and groom will need to get their lives going (no duplicates). The player with the most complete list is the winner. Now really concentrate because all game sheets will be given to the couple as a ''guide'' . . . to get them started!

You'll find a hint under each heading.

KITCHEN
Can Opener

LIVING ROOM
Picture Hangers

BEDROOM/BATH
Facial Tissue

TOOLS/HANDY ITEMS
Masking Tape

Let's Get the Couple Started!

Write down items, under each of the following headings, that the new bride and groom will need to get their lives going (no duplicates). The player with the most complete list is the winner. Now really concentrate because all game sheets will be given to the couple as a "guide" . . . to get them started!

You'll find a hint under each heading.

KITCHEN   **LIVING ROOM**

Can Opener   *Picture Hangers*

BEDROOM/BATH   **TOOLS/HANDY ITEMS**

Facial Tissue   *Masking Tape*

Let's Get the Couple Started!

Write down items, under each of the following headings, that the new bride and groom will need to get their lives going (no duplicates). The player with the most complete list is the winner. Now really concentrate because all game sheets will be given to the couple as a "guide" . . . to get them started!

You'll find a hint under each heading.

KITCHEN
Can Opener

LIVING ROOM
Picture Hangers

BEDROOM/BATH
Facial Tissue

TOOLS/HANDY ITEMS
Masking Tape

Let's Get the Couple Started!

Write down items, under each of the following headings, that the new bride and groom will need to get their lives going (no duplicates). The player with the most complete list is the winner. Now really concentrate because all game sheets will be given to the couple as a "guide" . . . to get them started!

You'll find a hint under each heading.

KITCHEN
Can Opener

LIVING ROOM
Picture Hangers

BEDROOM/BATH
Facial Tissue

TOOLS/HANDY ITEMS
Masking Tape

Let's Get the Couple Started!

Write down items, under each of the following headings, that the new bride and groom will need to get their lives going (no duplicates). The player with the most complete list is the winner. Now really concentrate because all game sheets will be given to the couple as a "guide" . . . to get them started!

You'll find a hint under each heading.

KITCHEN
Can Opener

LIVING ROOM
Picture Hangers

BEDROOM/BATH
Facial Tissue

TOOLS/HANDY ITEMS
Masking Tape

Let's Get the Couple Started!

Write down items, under each of the following headings, that the new bride and groom will need to get their lives going (no duplicates). The player with the most complete list is the winner. Now really concentrate because all game sheets will be given to the couple as a "guide" . . . to get them started!

You'll find a hint under each heading.

KITCHEN
Can Opener

LIVING ROOM
Picture Hangers

BEDROOM/BATH
Facial Tissue

TOOLS/HANDY ITEMS
Masking Tape

Let's Get the Couple Started!

Write down items, under each of the following headings, that the new bride and groom will need to get their lives going (no duplicates). The player with the most complete list is the winner. Now really concentrate because all game sheets will be given to the couple as a "guide" . . . to get them started!
You'll find a hint under each heading.

KITCHEN
Can Opener

LIVING ROOM
Picture Hangers

BEDROOM/BATH
Facial Tissue

TOOLS/HANDY ITEMS
Masking Tape

Let's Get the Couple Started!

Write down items, under each of the following headings, that the new bride and groom will need to get their lives going (no duplicates). The player with the most complete list is the winner. Now really concentrate because all game sheets will be given to the couple as a "guide" . . . to get them started!

You'll find a hint under each heading.

KITCHEN
Can Opener

LIVING ROOM
Picture Hangers

BEDROOM/BATH
Facial Tissue

TOOLS/HANDY ITEMS
Masking Tape

Let's Get the Couple Started!

Write down items, under each of the following headings, that the new bride and groom will need to get their lives going (no duplicates). The player with the most complete list is the winner. Now really concentrate because all game sheets will be given to the couple as a "guide" . . . to get them started!

You'll find a hint under each heading.

KITCHEN
Can Opener

LIVING ROOM
Picture Hangers

BEDROOM/BATH
Facial Tissue

TOOLS/HANDY ITEMS
Masking Tape

Let's Get the Couple Started!

Write down items, under each of the following headings, that the new bride and groom will need to get their lives going (no duplicates). The player with the most complete list is the winner. Now really concentrate because all game sheets will be given to the couple as a "guide" . . . to get them started!

You'll find a hint under each heading.

KITCHEN
Can Opener

LIVING ROOM
Picture Hangers

BEDROOM/BATH
Facial Tissue

TOOLS/HANDY ITEMS
Masking Tape

Let's Get the Couple Started!

Write down items, under each of the following headings, that the new bride and groom will need to get their lives going (no duplicates). The player with the most complete list is the winner. Now really concentrate because all game sheets will be given to the couple as a "guide" . . . to get them started!

You'll find a hint under each heading.

KITCHEN
Can Opener

LIVING ROOM
Picture Hangers

BEDROOM/BATH
Facial Tissue

TOOLS/HANDY ITEMS
Masking Tape

Showerwise Name Tags

Directions: Tear out sheet and cut along the outline of each name tag. If you wish to coordinate your shower colors, use thin-lined markers to decorate each name tag.

Showerwise Name Tags

Directions: Tear out sheet and cut along the outline of each name tag. If you wish to coordinate your shower colors, use thin-lined markers to decorate each name tag.

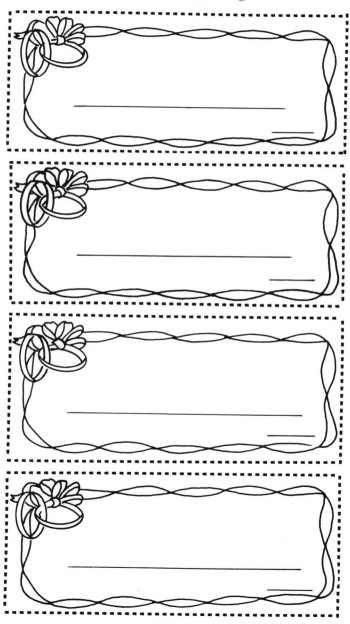

Showerwise Name Tags

Directions: Tear out sheet and cut along the outline of each name tag. If you wish to coordinate your shower colors, use thin-lined markers to decorate each name tag.

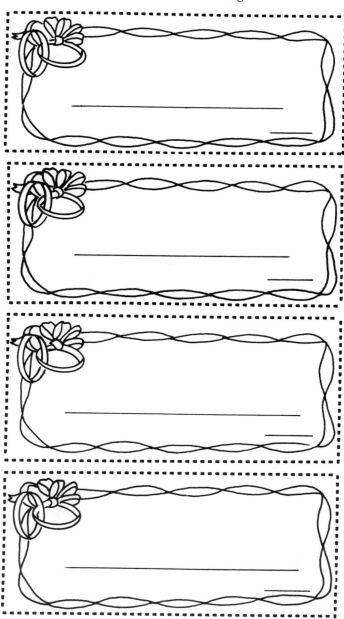

Answers To:

Courtship and Wedding Word-Puzzle

Starting Life Together

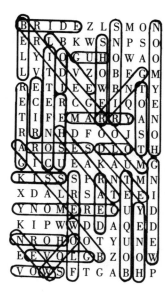

1. LOVE
2. SHARING
3. HUMOR
4. GIVING
5. CARING
6. FRIENDSHIP
7. FUN
8. ENCOURAGEMENT
9. PATIENCE
10. AFFECTION
11. TALKING
12. ADJUSTMENT
13. TRUST
14. GENEROSITY
15. FULFILLMENT
16. EQUALITY

Symbol Sayings

You gotta have heart. Sound as a bell. Gift of gab. Ring up the curtain. Kiss and tell. Hearts and flowers. You take the cake. Kissing don't last, cookery do. For whom the bells toll. To wear one's heart on one's sleeve. Ringling, Barnum & Bailey. A bell for Adano. It's not the gift, it's the thought. Flowers of the field. It's a piece of cake. Absence makes the heart grow fonder. Good sense is the gift of heaven. Ring around the collar. Cake walk. Say it with flowers. Peg 'O My Heart. Kissin' cousins. Belle of the ball. Love and kisses. Double ring ceremony.

Available from Brighton Publications, Inc.

Wedding Occasions: 101 New Party Themes for Wedding Showers, Rehearsal Dinners, Engagement Parties, and More! by Cynthia Lueck Sowden

Wedding Plans: 50 Unique Themes for the Wedding of Your Dreams by Sharon Dlugosch

Wedding Hints & Reminders by Sharon Dlugosch

Dream Weddings Do Come True: How to Plan a Stress-free Wedding by Cynthia Kreuger

Baby Shower Fun by Sharon Dlugosch

Games for Baby Shower Fun by Sharon Dlugosch

Kid-Tastic Birthday Parties: The Complete Party Planner for Today's Kids by Jane Chase

Romantic At-Home Dinners: Sneaky Strategies for Couples with Kids by Nan Booth/Gary Fischler

Reunions for Fun-Loving Families by Nancy Funke Bagley

An Anniversary to Remember: Years One to Seventy-five by Cynthia Lueck Sowden

Folding Table Napkins: A New Look at a Traditional Craft by Sharon Dlugosch

Table Setting Guide by Sharon Dlugosch

Tabletop Vignettes by Sharon Dlugosch

Don't Slurp Your Soup: A Basic Guide to Business Etiquette by Betty Craig

Meeting Room Games: Getting Things Done in Committees by Nan Booth

Hit the Ground Running: Communicate Your Way to Success by Cynthia Kreuger

These books are available in selected stores and catalogs. If you're having trouble finding them in your area, send a self-addressed, stamped, business-size envelope and request ordering information from:

Brighton Publications, Inc.
P.O. Box 120706
St. Paul, MN 55112-0706

or call: 1-800-536-BOOK